# YOUR KNOWLEDGE HAS VALUE

**Johannes Lenhard**

# What is kinship all about?

GRIN Verlag

**Bibliografische Information der Deutschen Nationalbibliothek:**

Die Deutsche Bibliothek verzeichnet diese Publikation in der Deutschen National-
bibliografie; detaillierte bibliografische Daten sind im Internet über http://dnb.d-
nb.de/ abrufbar.

**Imprint:**

Copyright © 2013 GRIN Verlag GmbH
Druck und Bindung: Books on Demand GmbH, Norderstedt Germany
ISBN: 978-3-656-46321-4

**This book at GRIN:**

http://www.grin.com/en/e-book/230431/what-is-kinship-all-about

**GRIN - Your knowledge has value**

Der GRIN Verlag publiziert seit 1998 wissenschaftliche Arbeiten von Studenten, Hochschullehrern und anderen Akademikern als eBook und gedrucktes Buch. Die Verlagswebsite www.grin.com ist die ideale Plattform zur Veröffentlichung von Hausarbeiten, Abschlussarbeiten, wissenschaftlichen Aufsätzen, Dissertationen und Fachbüchern.

**Visit us on the internet:**

http://www.grin.com/

http://www.facebook.com/grincom

http://www.twitter.com/grin_com

# What is kinship all about?

Kinship is grounded in biological facts. It is based on the undeniable, universal reality of biological rules – a child is related to two parents of different sex – and concerned about how sociological structures – who cares for the child? – map on to this. This view of kinship as the hard science of biology for a long time had ardent supporters, Morgan and Gellner among them. The exceptions – adoption for instance – that even Morgan and Gellner admitted to this rule of 'biology only' soon took got the upper hand. However, alternatives were not immediately at hand. Needham and after him Schneider argued for the death of kinship as a whole while already very early Durkheim and Rivers search for a solution in a recourse to 'social kinship'. It took another couple of decades, however, until scholars such as Bloch/Guggenheim and Clarke fully developed a repertoire for analysing social kinship in terms of for instance nurture and care. Problematic in all those accounts was merely one thing: they did not deal with the dichotomy between nature and culture, between biological and social kinship. Carstens tries to address this shortcoming with her more dynamic notion of 'relatedness' mapped onto Latourian networks. The final question, however, remains: are we really developing towards a 'hybrid idea' if kinship between biological and social relations?

Kinship – what one might call a bond between people creating obligations and rights beyond friendship – is based on biology. 'True parenthood' has its roots in natural facts, in the facts of birth, cohabitation and blood. The early school of kinship studies, among others **Morgan** (1880/1997) claims that it is the 'system of consanguinity', of blood, which is the formal expression and recognition of these relationships. For him, kinship essentially consists of the social recognition of biological facts clearly establishing a privileged position for the 'natural basis of life'. His conception of marriage as the 'sexual relationship between male and female' exemplifies this belief unequivocally. Even though already at Morgan's time, non-biological concepts such as adoption were fairly common, this underlying basis of kinship in biology was not challenged. As Schneider recapitulates (1987:97) "biological relationship was treated as the reference point, the fixed position against which all cultural aspects take their meaning". Adoption was an exception that was always defined with reference to the norm of biology, always 'singled out'.

**Gellner** (1987) is the most prominent advocate of this school until very late in the 1980s. For him, the crucial question for an anthropologist interested in kinship is "under what conditions will the anthropologist's treatment of the blip-relationship fall under the rubric of kinship structure?" (ibid.:163). The only legitimate answer for him is to be seen in the overlap with physical kinship relationships. Also he does not claim that this rule holds up for every relation (e.g. consequences of undetected infidelity, godparents) that might be defined as kinship. However, kinship and descent systems are 'functions' of physical kinship: "kinship structure means the manner in which a pattern of physical relationships is made use of for social purposes" (ibid.:170). Kinship is as such based on purely biological rules such as the rules governing 'mating'. Methodologically, Gellner raises an important point as well: it is not so much about how people perceive their kin relationships; kinship should be used as a comparative-analytical category defined and applied by the anthropologist. Biological and natural truths are given to the analyst so that "sociological accounts of social relationships such as marriage involves plotting their relationships against existing physical facts" (ibid.:175). Those biological truths can not be challenged – they are universally underlying every discussion on kinship.

In a direct reply to Gellner, Rodney **Needham** (1974) denounces the former's preoccupation with biological kinship as both methodologically and factually wrong. The search for generalisation and the blind belief in a positive natural-social science has to be overcome. Relating back to Leach's 'Rethinking Anthropology', Needham advocates individual rather than general understanding of different cultures in their own right. For kinship studies, this has radical consequences. When he opens up the definition of kinship as the "allocation of rights and their transmission from one generation to the next" (ibid.:40) referring to rights of group membership, inheritance of property, locality of residence and type of occupation, he agrees on hollowing it out. The word is devoid of meaning; there is no such thing as kinship left if it includes such a diversity of phenomena as "segmentary organisation, section-systems, widow inheritance, polyandry, teknonymy, divorce rates" (ibid.:42). Needham in this way foreshadows Schneider. Rather than the attachment to "inappropriate conceptions of a class" possessing certain attributes ('butterfly collecting') and the search for sociological laws in a hard-science fashion, Needham wants anthropology to step back:

> "It may be that all social anthropology will be able to do ... is to comprehend, in one case after another, the schemes in which men of different cultures have variously taken advantage of logical and psychic facilities which are the elementary resources available to all mankind in the ordering of experience" (ibid.:71)

He finds a solution in the recourse to 'logical laws' while – just as Leach – not defining (and demonstrating in detail) what this means. Can it, however, be a way out to loose interest in kinship altogether?

**Scheffler and Lounsbury** (1971) propose a different answer that still grapples with Gellner's legacy. Not abandoning the focus on 'biology', they don't want to dismiss kinship as a whole, but rather define it in folk theory terms. Kinship should be about *their* theory of reproduction. Putting 'shared' components, such as the body, bones, flesh and blood into a more prominent position, the preoccupation with biology decouples from Western beliefs towards native's ideas about conception and birth. Malinowski's (1929) account of the 'naïve Trobrianders' can be seen as a major example: he finds that they have a theory of conception based on spirit reincarnation. Sexual contact does not play a role in this explanation rendering 'biological fatherhood' obsolete. Essentially, this 'sticky' focus on biology is part of what Schneider (1987) calls the 'Genealogical Unity of Manking'-assumption. A particular generation of anthropologists built on the assumption that all human cultures believe in human reproduction and biological relatedness; those categorisation are furthermore comparable, but culminate in an abstract genealogy applicable to all human cultures" (ibid.:120).

**Schneider** (1987:189ff) concludes that the source for this seemingly unalterable biological bias can be found in a fundamentally Western assumption: 'blood is thicker than water'. The social sciences – and the social scientist – are often not able to purify their own research: "It is simply that so much what passes for science in the social sciences ... derives directly and recognisably from the commonsense notions, the everyday premises of the culture in which and by which the scientist lives" (ibid.:175). Kinship is a metacultural categor[y] embedded in European culture which ha[s] been incorporated into the analytic schemes of European social scientists" (ibid.:184). Therefore, kinship does not deserve such a prominent place – particularly not in comparative studies of non-euro-american countries – because it merely is a category of Western thought, so Schneider. Scholars have proposed a less radical alternative to 'dropping out of kinship' – the consideration of other, mainly social, sources of kinship.

That kinship-relations are not merely based on the social recognition of biological facts has already been debated in the beginning of the twentieth century. **Durkheim** (1898) goes as far as to claim that the early forms of kinship groups were mostly 'totally independent' of consanguineal ties. Much more it was the (immaterial) descendancy from one and the same totem or particular signs (tattooing, food prohibitions, blood communion) that defined kin relations – in addition to birth. Kinship is inherently social consisting of jural and moral relations sanctioned by society. Those laws and sanctions – customs – according to **Thomas** (1906/2010) determine the limits in which consanguinity is supposed to exist rather than the other way round. By the turn of the 20<sup>th</sup> Century, the conception of kinship as purely biological had already declined. Durkheim, Rivers, van Gennep and Rivers had introduced promising starting point distinguishing physical and social bases for kinship already decoupling certain facts of sociological kinship. **Rivers** even directly denounces the notion of consanguinity as definitory criterion for kinship relations: "nearly all ... peoples of the world preserve, either in writing or in their memories a record of those with thom they are related by consanguinity or by those social conventions which, as we have seen, serve the same social purpose" (in Schneider, 1987:105). During his own fieldwork in the Bank Islands, Rivers found examples of social kinship established merely by paying the midwife. Again, his advances could have radically challenged dominant notions of kinship but were also in his own work rather marginal and not able to attack genealogy as the defining feature of kinship. His genealogies were still based on parent-child paths - imposing the 'english sense' of fatherhood as a consanguineal relation. The meaning of terms such as father, sister, mother still was taken to be self-evident so that kinship remained intricately tied to biology – due to a lack of clear alternative examples. For this early generation of sociologists and anthropologists, three problems prevailed: they lacked specification in what a 'social' alternative to biological ties would consist of while at the same time not caring enough for the relationship between social and physical ties. Thirdly, in practical terms, their research was often 'feeble' and not following their own theoretical achievements. As Schneider (1987:123) rightly sums up: "it is assumed that this relationship, of birth or blood or biological relatedness ... is ... privileged".

Compadrazgo – "the links established between parents and godparents in Catholic societies" (Bloch & Guggenheim, 1981:376)– can be seen as a step further away from the focus on biological ties. Filed under the category of 'spiritual' (as opposed to natural) kinship, Compadrazgo challenges the 'natural presumption'. Compadrazgo rituals and their effects are often modelled on kinship but don't involve as many material obligations and responsibilities as 'true kinship'; the focus is on spiritual – "from the state of Original Sin to the state of grace" (ibid.:378) – and religious life. Baptism consists of a metaphorical cleansing devaluing natural birth, women in general and the mother in particular; it is "a ritual denying the woman's ability to produce socially acceptable children" (ibid.:380). With case material from the Merina of Madagascar, Bloch and Guggenheim introduce the notion of 'alternative, community-appointed parents' with the context of a circumcision ceremony for boys. Just as in Compadrazgo, the ideological core can be found in the "denial of biological birth … replacing it with a ritual re-enactment of birth" (ibid.:384). Even though "the role of the godparent … is not simply that of substitute parent" but rather an "intermediary…who have been given the power to be parents from on high, whether from the Church, the State or the ancestors", this social notion of kinship has to be acknowledged as challenging to a high degree the above ideas.

A second example for this most recent advance in notions of 'social kinship' is provided by **Clarke's** (2008) account of Muslim notions of kinship. In the Lebanon, many cases of elective and non-biogenetic kinship are constructed in secrecy still paying attention to Muslim morality. In a context of secular and liberal thinking, values such as 'honour', 'shame' and 'reputation' remain of enduring importance – at least on the outset. The underlying (private) practices already breath the air of 'western cultural freedom', in this case particularly sexual freedom. Nevertheless, ideas about kinship are still tied together in both spheres: "Not all biological children can legitimately claim *nasab*: the bastard is … denied paternal relations in Sunni thought, and paternal and maternal relations in Shiite thought" (ibid.:163). Clarke therefore claims that there is "no classical concept of a 'natural' child" (ibid.). Parenthood in Lebanon can be characterised as being based on claims of legitimation – rather than natural facts.

One might argue that even the more recent accounts of Clarke and Bloch/Guggenheim do not deal with a major flaw that already Schneider (1987:189ff) describes. Neither accounts arguing for the criticalness of biological relatedness nor those proposing an alternative in socially configured relations overcome the distinction between biological and social kinship. Even though the acknowledgment of social facts already constitutes an important step away from a prejudiced Western conception of kinship as biology, also newer accounts struggle with relating the two spheres elegantly without recourse to arguments of causation or mirroring.

Rather than separating off the two spheres and analysing their potential relationship, **Carstens** (2000) argues for a 'new unity'. Acknowledging that biological facts do not have universal significance, Carstens and her followers open up the definition of kinship towards 'relatedness' not relying on an 'arbitrary distinction' between biology and culture. Particularly building on Strathern's (1992) work, the effects of technological developments – new reproductive technologies, such as in-vitro-fertilisation or surrogate mothers – force the domain of kinship in a hybrid-status between nature-and-culture. Taking into consideration the 'technological turn', Strathern characterises kinship as the 'construction and cultivation of social relations 'out of' or 'after' natural properties and natural relations" (Faubion, 1996:87). "Scientific facts are as much made as they are discovered" (Carstens, 2000:11). Even if it is surprising that it took the recent technological developments to make anthropology properly recognise the fact that 'kinship is not given', this denaturalisation is now undeniable. I would not follow Faubion (1997) to the very end, proclaiming the complete demise of nature as an underlying factor in kinship relations, but we have to admit its confusion. In her own fieldwork with Malay people, Carstens (1997) demonstrates how kinship is influenced both by ties of procreation and through everyday acts of nurture, care and hospitality. Hutchinson (Hutchinson, 2000) makes a similar argument in her study about the Nuer: "Nuer use of not only blood and other bodily substances but also food, soil, cattle, paper, money and guns to invoke and to rupture bonds of relatedness". Even though biology (birth, conception) do indeed provide *one* basis for kinship claims, feeding and the consumption of food can be of equal importance. No one explanation is to be preferred but several possibilities can work potentially even at the same time. "What emerges from this analysis is that there is a combination of sentiment, substance, and nurturance as grounds for relatedness." (ibid.:22). Carstens goes beyond Schneider in this respect searching for a dynamic form of kinship. She finds a model for this in Latour's (1993) notion of (actor)networks enabling the combination of social and biological elements, as well as human and non-human material. On a more abstract level, this conception of kinship as a 'network' refers to an underlying concept of the human person as a 'dividual' (Strathern, 1998). Personhood is inherently multiple – Gudeman (1972) argues dual – as well as dynamically transformative through performances and practices. There is no single defining criterion, but rather a multiple range of potential influences – particularly when it comes to kinship.

So, kinship has arrived now. Having started from a biological – arguably Western – point of view defining kinship as the natural (blood) relations between for instance parents and children, anthropologists found a way to introduce social kinship into the picture first. Even though it took a while to really define what might be meant by that – care and nurture – particularly the NRT have eventually challenged the primate of biology in the study of kinship. Finally, also the static dichotomy between nature and culture has come under attack by a more dynamic notion of 'relatedness'. Even though, I am not able to judge in conclusion where this concept has developed since it was first introduced into the discourse roughly 10 years ago, it does not really seemed to have solved the problems that still prevailed for kinship. What is it actually, that Carstens and her followers mean? What does it mean that kinship is a 'hybrid between biology and culture'? Isn't Clarke right claiming that there is nothing 'new' about 'new kinship studies'? Clarke (2008) actually also found a new – or rather old – turn in at least Muslim kinship: rather than developing towards more 'hybridity' – between social and biological, between moral and natural – kinship in Lebanon undergoes an overwhelming 'modernist influence'. "A previously important part of kinship's social component – concern over the propriety of the sexual relationship through which the child was conceived, has disappeared from sight" (ibid.:2008:165). Does that mean that we are going back to nature, back to biology? If even the 'East' is now taking over a Western notion of kinship based on biology, where do developments like NRT lead? Will a more progressive development towards 'hybridity' as promoted by Carstens become obsolete, become overruled by a new over-dominance of 'assisted biology'?

**List of references**

Bloch, M., & Guggenheim, S. (1981). Compadrazgo, Baptism and the Symbolism of a Second Birth. *Man, 16*(3), 376–386.

Carstens, J. (1997). *The Heat of the Hearth: The process of Kinship in a Malay Fishing Community.* Oxford: Clarendon Press.

Carstens, J. (2000). *Cultures of Relatedness: New Approaches to the Study of Kinship.* Cambridge: Cambridge University Press.

Clarke, M. (2008). New kinship, Islam, and the liberal tradition: sexual morality and new reproductive technology in Lebanon. *Journal of the Royal anthropological Institute, 14*, 153–169.

Faubion, J. D. (1996). Kinship is Dead . Long Live Kinship. A Review Article. *Comparative Studies in Society and History, 38*(1), 67–91.

Gellner, E. (1987). *The Concept of Kinship: And Other Essays on Anthropological Method and Explanation:* Oxford: Basil Blackwell.

Gudeman, S. (1972). The compadrazgo as a reflection of the spiritual and natural person. *Proceedings of the Royal Anthropological Institute,* 1971, 45-71.

Hutchinson, S. (2000). Identity and substance: the broadening bases of relatedness among the Nuer of southern Sudan. In J. Carstens (Ed.), *Cultures of Relatedness* (pp. 55–73). Cambridge: Cambridge University Press.

Latour, B. (1993). *We Have Never Been Modern* (p. 168). Cambridge (MA): Harvard University Press.

Malinowski, B. (1929). *The Sexual Life of Savages.* London: Routledge.

Morgan, L. (1997). *Systems of consanguinity and affinity of the human family*. Omaha: University of Nebraska Press.

Needham, R. (1974). *Remarks and Inventions: Skeptical Essays About Kinship*. London: Tavistock Publications.

Scheffler, H. W., & Lounsbury, F. G. (1971). *A study in structural semantics: the Siriono kinship system*. London: Prentice-Hall.

Schneider, D. M. (1987). *A Critique of the Study of Kinship*. Ann Arbour: University of Michigan Press.

Strathern, M. (1992). *After Nature: English Kinship in the Late Twentieth Century*. Cambridge: Cambridge University Press.

Thomas, N. W. (2010). *Kinship Organisations and Group Marriage in Australia* (p. 188). Cambridge: Cambridge University Press.